A DREAM COME TRUE

by

Johanna Hurwitz

photographs by

Michael Craine

 Richard C. Owen Publishers, Inc.
Katonah, New York

Meet the Author titles

Verna Aardema *A Bookworm Who Hatched*
David A. Adler *My Writing Day*
Frank Asch *One Man Show*
Joseph Bruchac *Seeing the Circle*
Eve Bunting *Once Upon a Time*
Lynne Cherry *Making a Difference in the World*
Lois Ehlert *Under My Nose*
Jean Fritz *Surprising Myself*
Paul Goble *Hau Kola Hello Friend*
Ruth Heller *Fine Lines*
Lee Bennett Hopkins *The Writing Bug*
James Howe *Playing with Words*
Johanna Hurwitz *A Dream Come True*

Karla Kuskin *Thoughts, Pictures, and Words*
Thomas Locker *The Man Who Paints Nature*
Jonathan London *Tell Me a Story*
George Ella Lyon *A Wordful Child*
Margaret Mahy *My Mysterious World*
Rafe Martin *A Storyteller's Story*
Patricia McKissack *Can You Imagine?*
Patricia Polacco *Firetalking*
Laurence Pringle *Nature! Wild and Wonderful*
Cynthia Rylant *Best Wishes*
Seymour Simon *From Paper Airplanes to Outer Space*
Jean Van Leeuwen *Growing Ideas*
Jane Yolen *A Letter from Phoenix Farm*

Text copyright © 1998 by Johanna Hurwitz
Photographs copyright © 1998 by Michael Craine

Richard C. Owen Publishers, Inc.
PO Box 585
Katonah, New York 10536

Library of Congress Cataloging-in-Publication Data

Hurwitz, Johanna.
     A dream come true / by Johanna Hurwitz ; photographs by Michael Craine.
         p .   cm . — (Meet the author)
     Summary: A prominent children's book author shares her life, her daily activities, and her creative process, showing how all are intertwined.
     ISBN 1-57274-193-7 (hardcover)
     1. Hurwitz, Johanna—Biography—Juvenile literature.
2. Authors, American—20th century—Biography—Juvenile literature.
3. Children's literature—Authorship— Juvenile literature.
[1. Hurwitz, Johanna. 2. Women authors. 3. Illustrators. Women—Biography.]
I. Craine, Michael, ill. II. Title. III. Series: Meet the author (Katonah, N.Y.)
PS3558.U697Z464 1998
813' .54—dc21
[B]   98-9371

Editorial, Art, and Production Director *Janice Boland*
Production Assistants *Donna Parsons* and *Marc Caroul*
Color separations by Leo P. Callahan Inc., Binghamton, NY

Printed in the United States of America

9 8 7 6 5 4 3 2

For my readers
May your dreams come true

I had a secret dream.

Ever since I was young, I wanted to be a writer.

When I was growing up I made up tales
and told them to my little brother.

I wrote stories and made my own little booklets.

One was even illustrated by a classmate.

A favorite book of mine was *Heidi*
by Johanna Spyri. I liked seeing my first name,
Johanna, on the cover of the book.
I'd put my hand over the name Spyri
and try to imagine what it would be like
if both of my names were on the book.

My family lived in the Bronx,
New York. When I was ten, I wrote a poem
which was published in a newspaper.

"Books"
For me to read a book is still
And always will be quite a thrill.
For me to read a book is like
A boy when he rides his new two wheel bike.
And when a bird comes north in spring
It's natural for him to sing.
I like to read books of science, fiction,
        and mystery;
Books of poems, nature, and history.
And what is more, I'll read until I'm grown,
And then I'll write books of my own.

I received a check for fifty cents as payment.
Fifty cents wasn't very much money.
Still, I was proud to see my words
and my name in print.

My first book wasn't published until I was
a grown woman. By then I was married
to Uri Hurwitz and had two children, Nomi and Beni.

That first book, *Busybody Nora*,
was all about the four of us and our life
in a New York City apartment building.

Working as a librarian in New York City and caring
for my family took time. However, in the evening
after my children were asleep, I sat and wrote
stories at the kitchen table.

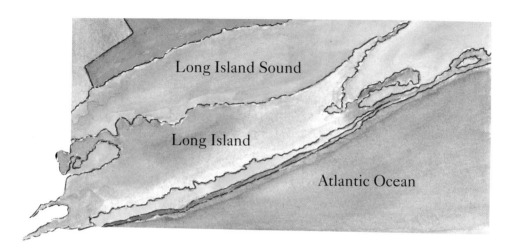

Long Island Sound

Long Island

Atlantic Ocean

When we moved to a house on Long Island
I picked out a room of my own in which I could
write. It would be my study. The door was always
open to my family. After all, my best story ideas
came from the things they said and did.

Now my children are grown up.
But I still write about little Nora and Teddy
and their friends Russell and Elisa.

I write about lots of other children, too.
There's Lucas Cott, who is a class clown,
and Cricket Kaufman, the teacher's pet.
There's Aldo Applesauce and Ali Baba Bernstein,
Adam Fine, who has a llama in his family,
and Ezra Feldman, who has baseball fever.

There is also Rory, Derek, and Bolivia,
who are in *The Hot & Cold Summer*
and my books about the other seasons.

"Which character are you?" boys and girls ask me.
The truth is that a little bit of me is in every
character. "Which book is your favorite?" they
want to know. It's impossible for me to choose.
For each book is special in its own way.

Most of my days begin with a morning walk.
Walking is important for my body.
It's important for my writing, too.
As I go down the street,
I talk to myself and my characters.
I figure out what I will write next.
Sometimes I get great ideas!

Once I found a wristwatch.

I didn't keep it, but it gave me the idea
to give one just like it to Ozzie Sims in my book
Ozzie on His Own. Another time I found a fifty
dollar bill. That got into a story, too.

But in my story I turned it into a hundred dollar
bill. That's part of the fun of being a writer of
fiction. You can change things however you wish.

After my walk, I have breakfast.
Then it's time to write. I go to my study
and start off by writing a letter to a friend.
It's my warm-up exercise.
Often Uri comes in the room to talk with me.
Sometimes the phone rings. I don't mind
being interrupted because I know I can always
get back to my work.

When you read one of my books,
it should feel as if the words of my story
just flowed from my thoughts onto the paper.

That isn't true. I struggle to put my words down
on the page. I write and rewrite, and rewrite again.
Sometimes I change the order of the chapters.
Sometimes I add a new character or make one
disappear. Sometimes in the middle of a story
I change everyone's names.

I love names. I have a drawer filled with pieces of paper with names. I need names for my characters, and names for their schools and the streets and shops that will be in the story. I "borrow" names from the boys and girls whose books I autograph, from the children who write me letters, from friends, and from family members.

Sometimes I find a good name when I'm reading the newspaper or the phone book. When I begin a new book, I take all the names from my drawer and decide which ones I'll use.

Wherever I go, I carry a small notebook.
When I get an idea, see something that catches my
attention, or hear something funny, I write it down.

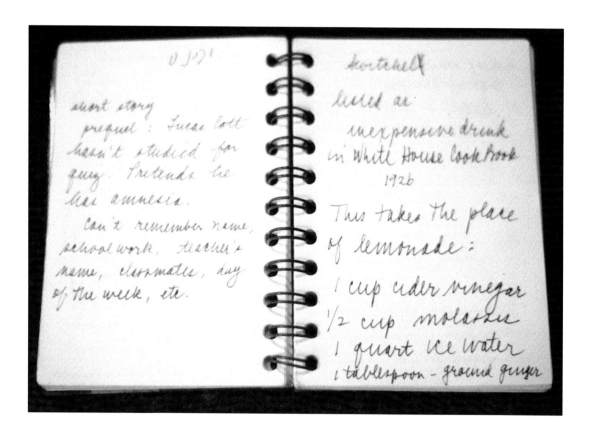

My desk is filled with these small notebooks.
And each notebook is filled with story ideas.

Though most of my books are fiction, I often do research. When I met a woman who owned a pair of llamas, I thought it would be fun to write about owning a llama.

I wrote a few sentences in my notebook.

I read about llamas, visited a llama farm, and went on a llama trek in the mountains of Vermont.

I jotted down many new pieces of information
in my notebook. Soon I was ready to begin writing
my story. I called it *A Llama in the Family*.

When I wrote
The Rabbi's Girls, which
is about my mother's
childhood, I wanted to
learn about life in the
1920s, so I read back
issues of old newspapers.

When I wrote
Baseball Fever
I took a trip to
Cooperstown,
New York, to visit the
Baseball Hall of Fame.

Before I write, I know how my story will begin.
I know how it will end.
But what will happen in the middle
is always a big surprise.
As I write, I learn about my characters
from the conversations they have.
Sometimes they do unexpected things
and my story changes.

For example, I didn't know that Aldo would
become a vegetarian in *Much Ado About Aldo*.

I write every day until one o'clock.
I stop for lunch. And in the afternoon
I take care of my mail.

I write to the boys and girls and teachers
who have been reading my stories.
They send me their photographs and drawings.
They tell me how much they liked my books.

In the evening I sit and read.
Our cat Sinbad climbs onto my lap
and purrs. Selena, our other cat, sits nearby.
Uri sits across the room reading a book, too.
Sometimes Uri reads something from his book
to me. And sometimes I read something from my
book to him.

In the summer, we go off to Vermont.
I walk in the woods and enjoy nature.
There, too, I do a lot of writing
in a room of my own.

I never dreamed that because of my books,
I would be invited to visit schools and libraries
all over the world.

I love seeing new places and learning
about different cultures.

But the most wonderful thing is seeing
over and over again that children haven't changed.
Children all over the world are so very much like
I was when I was a child,
and so very much like my children were
when they were little.

When I come home and unpack my suitcase,
I can't wait to sit at my desk and get to work
on my next story.

I feel very lucky that my dream
of writing books of my own has come true.

Johanna Hurwitz

Other Books by Johanna Hurwitz

Aldo Applesauce; Class Clown; Leonard Bernstein: A Passion for Music; New Shoes for Silvia; Ever-Clever Eliza; Roz and Ozzie; Russell Sprouts; Super Duper Teddy

About the Photographer

Michael Craine studied photography to learn the technique and the art of creating beautiful and interesting photographs of people and the things they do. Michael spent two days with Johanna Hurwitz taking pictures of all the things she does to create her stories. He also spent several days with the author James Howe, taking pictures for his autobiography *Playing with Words*.

Acknowledgments

Photographs on pages 4, 5, 8, 10, 11, 19 (top), and 28 courtesy of Johanna Hurwitz. Photographs on pages 19 (bottom) and 20 by Janice Boland. Illustration on page 6 from *Heidi* by Johanna Spyri, illustrated by Agnes Tait, copyright © 1948 by J. B. Lippincott Co. Used by permission of HarperCollins Publishers, Inc. Illustration on page 9 from *Busybody Nora* by Johanna Hurwitz, illustrated by Susan Jeschke. Illustrations copyright © 1976 by Susan Jeschke. By permission of Morrow Junior Books, a division of William Morrow & Company Inc. Illustration on page 11 from *Nora and Mrs. Mind-Your-Own-Business* by Johanna Hurwitz, illustrated by Lillian Hoban. Illustrations copyright © 1977 by Lillian Hoban. By permission of Morrow Junior Books, a division of William Morrow & Company, Inc. Illustration on page 12 from *The Hot & Cold Summer* by Johanna Hurwitz, illustrated by Gail Owens. Illustrations copyright © 1984 by Gail Owens. By permission of Morrow Junior Books, a division of William Morrow & Company Inc. Illustration on page 20 from *A Llama in the Family* by Johanna Hurwitz, illustrated by Mark Graham. Illustrations copyright © 1994 by Mark Graham. By permission of Morrow Junior Books, a division of William Morrow & Company Inc. Illustration on page 21 (top) from *The Rabbi's Girls* by Johanna Hurwitz, Copyright © 1982 by Johanna Hurwitz. Illustrated by Pamela Johnson. By permission of Morrow Junior Books, a division of William Morrow & Company Inc. Illustration on page 21 (bottom) from *Baseball Fever* by Johanna Hurwitz, © 1981 by Johanna Hurwitz. Illustrated by Ray Cruz. By permission of Morrow Junior Books, a division of William Morrow & Company Inc. Illustration on page 22 from *Much Ado About Aldo* by Johanna Hurwitz, Copyright © 1978 by Johanna Hurwitz. Illustrated by John Wallner. By permission of Morrow Junior Books, a division of William Morrow & Company Inc. Photo on page 28 by Uri Hurwitz. Photo on back cover by Johanna Mustacchi